Crushing Avalanches

Louise and Richard Spilsbury

www.heinemann.co.uk/library
Visit our website to find out more information about **Heinemann Library** books.

To order:
 Phone 44 (0) 1865 888066
 Send a fax to 44 (0) 1865 314091
 Visit the Heinemann Bookshop at www.heinemann.co.uk/library to browse our catalogue and order online.

First published in Great Britain by Heinemann Library, Halley Court, Jordan Hill, Oxford OX2 8EJ, part of Harcourt Education.
Heinemann is a registered trademark of Harcourt Education Ltd.

Editorial: Andrew Farrow and Dan Nunn
Design: David Poole and Paul Myerscough
Illustrations: Geoff Ward
Picture Research: Rebecca Sodergren and Debra Weatherley
Production: Edward Moore

Originated by Dot Gradations Limited
Printed in Hong Kong, China by Wing King Tong

ISBN 0 431 17831 3
07 06 05 04 03
10 9 8 7 6 5 4 3 2 1

British Library Cataloguing in Publication Data
Spilsbury, Richard, 1963 –
Crushing avalanches. – (Awesome Forces of Nature)
1. Avalanches – Juvenile literature
I. Title II. Spilsbury, Louise
551.3'07
A full catalogue record for this book is available from the British Library.

Acknowledgements
The publishers would like to thank the following for permission to reproduce photographs:

Alamy p. **12**; AP pp. **5** (Lechiner), **16** (Georg Koechler), **17** (Douglas C. Pizac), **18** (Dietner Endlicher), **19** (Rudi Blaha); Corbis pp. **11**, **13**, **21**, **26**; Das Fotoarchive p. **22** (Marcus Matzel), **27**; Eric Limon Photography p. **14**; Rex Features pp. **15** (SIPA Press), **25** (Toby Rankin); South American Pictures p. **10**; SPL p. **7**; Still Pictures pp. **4** (Roberta Parkin), **24** (Andreas Riedmiller); Trip pp. **23** (Mountain Sport), **28** (Ask Images); Venture Pix p. **8**; Yoram Porath p. **9**.

Cover photograph reproduced with permission of Roberta Parkin/Still Pictures.

Every effort has been made to contact copyright holders of any material reproduced in this book. Any omissions will be rectified in subsequent printings if notice is given to the publishers.

Contents

*Any words appearing in the text in bold, **like this**, are explained in the Glossary.*

What is an avalanche?

When snow slides or slips down mountainsides we call it an avalanche. The word avalanche comes from a French word that means 'descent' or fall. As the snow slides down, it bashes into ice, rocks, soil and trees. If it hits them with enough force, they come hurtling down the mountain too.

When do avalanches happen?

There are many avalanches every year, usually at the same times of year. They can only happen after snow has fallen and collected on mountainsides during cold seasons. Most avalanches in Europe and North America happen between January and March.

Some happen later in the year, when temperatures start to get warmer and the snow and ice start to thaw. In these conditions, big chunks of snow do not stick to the ground very well and may start to move.

An avalanche like this can come racing down a mountainside without any warning. Eyewitnesses say that a speeding mass of ice and snow like this sounds like a roaring thunderstorm.

Destructive forces

Avalanches vary in size and force. They can be slow movements of a few kilograms of snow over a few metres. They can also be massive shifts of hundreds of tonnes of snow and rock. These speed for several kilometres down a mountainside, like express trains.

Big avalanches can destroy anything that gets in their way. In some places big avalanches knock down trees and affect the lives of mountain animals. In other places they can crush whole towns and the people who live there. In these places, avalanches become terrible natural disasters.

An avalanche can bury cars, buildings, roads, animals and people under a heavy blanket of icy snow.

AVALANCHE FACTS

! There are perhaps a million avalanches each year around the world; most cause very little damage to people.

! Avalanches can move at up to 300 kilometres per hour – that is the speed of a Formula One racing car. They usually move much faster than any person can run.

Where do avalanches happen?

Avalanches happen all over the world where snow falls and there are mountains. Many of the avalanches that take place go unnoticed by people because they happen in remote snowy places where nobody goes. Some avalanches affect people who live on or at the edge of mountain ranges. Mountain ranges where there are lots of avalanches include the Alps in Europe, the Himalayas in Nepal and Tibet (in Asia), the Andes in South America, and the Rocky Mountains in the USA.

Avalanches often happen in exactly the same locations within these mountain areas. This is because only certain slopes are steep enough for snow to settle and to slide down.

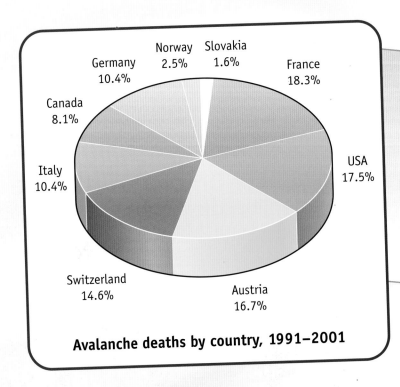

Avalanche deaths by country, 1991–2001

Germany 10.4%
Norway 2.5%
Slovakia 1.6%
France 18.3%
Canada 8.1%
Italy 10.4%
USA 17.5%
Switzerland 14.6%
Austria 16.7%

*Over 1300 people died in avalanches between 1991 and 2001. This **pie chart** shows that most deaths resulting from avalanches happened in France, Austria and the USA.*

What causes an avalanche?

Snow that has already fallen and built up on a slope is called **snow cover**. Most snow cover is stable, which means it stays where it is on a slope. But some snow cover is unstable and this may start an avalanche.

Types of snow cover

Snow falls from the sky as star-shaped flakes or as rounded granules, depending on the temperature. After snow lands it changes shape because of the weight of more snow landing on top of it and because of temperature changes. This is called settling. When flakes settle they form stable snow cover, but granules roll over each other, and settle as weak layers of snow. If a lot of snow falls quickly on top of a weak layer – for example in a **blizzard**, or when thick, heavy **snowdrifts** form in heavy winds – then it may form unstable snow cover. Avalanches are **triggered** by slight movements of unstable snow cover.

Snowflakes settle to form stable snow cover because their points lock together like pieces of a jigsaw puzzle.

Triggers

Sometimes small movements can trigger an avalanche, such as the movement of a wild animal or the melting of a layer of snow. Some avalanches are caused by the shaking force of a loud machine or even an earthquake. However, most fatal avalanches are triggered by people.

Are all avalanches the same?

Not all avalanches are the same. There are four main types, depending on snow cover: dry slab, wet slab, wind and ice.

Dry **slab avalanches** are most common. Layers of settled snow build up to form a thick, dry snow slab which can become as brittle as a pane of glass. When triggered, it can suddenly shatter and break into big chunks of ice that slide down mountainsides at high speeds.

Wet slab avalanches happen when rain and sun weaken large slabs of snow cover. They slip down the mountainside much more slowly than shattered hard slabs. As they are wet and heavy, they drag boulders, trees and soil along with them.

Dry slab avalanches slip like fast sledges over the weak snow layer underneath.

Wind avalanches are less common. Occasionally snow falls and settles as a mixture of flakes and granules, forming a loose, light powder. When an avalanche is triggered, the powder forms giant snowclouds. These snowclouds travel down slopes very quickly, creating a ferocious wind ahead of them.

Ice avalanches are rare, but they have caused some of the worst avalanche disasters. **Glaciers** are immense slabs of ice that form on shallow slopes after years of snowfall. They usually move really slowly because they are so heavy. Sometimes huge chunks of glacier can break off and start an ice avalanche. They may move fast, sweeping hundreds of tonnes of snow, rock, soil or water in front of them.

When ice avalanches fall into water, they can cause big, destructive waves.

Yungay, Peru, 1970

Yungay is a small town in the Andes mountains, in Peru. On the afternoon of 31 May 1970, many of the town's people were listening to the soccer World Cup on the radio. At 3.23 p.m. a huge earthquake shook most of Peru. Walls and houses crumpled and whole streets split open. But this destructive force was just the beginning – it also triggered an awesome **ice avalanche**.

Falling mountain

Mount Huascarán – the tallest mountain in Peru – is nearly 7 kilometres high. It is at one end of a high-sided valley containing Yungay and several villages. Before the earthquake, a **glacier**, high on Huascarán, had been weakened as it thawed during the spring. When the earthquake hit, it shook loose a piece of the glacier.

'At that time I heard a great roar coming from Huascarán. Looking up, I saw what appeared to be a cloud of dust and it looked as though a large mass of rock and ice was breaking loose from the north peak.' Mateo Casaverde, survivor

The centre of Yungay in 1968. These palm trees survived the avalanche in 1970.

Speeding wave

The ice avalanche was around 1 kilometre across and weighed millions of tonnes. It dropped nearly 4 kilometres before it hit the valley floor. It then hurtled down the valley towards Yungay, pushing an immense wave of snow, rock, soil and water in front of it.

'The crest of the wave had a curl, like a huge breaker coming in from the ocean. I estimated the wave to be at least 80 metres high. I reached the high ground of the cemetery a few seconds before the debris flow struck the base of the hill.' Mateo Casaverde

The wave took about 3 minutes to travel 15 kilometres to Yungay. The town was completely buried by the avalanche. Of the town's 25,000 inhabitants, only around 2000 survived. It was the world's worst recorded avalanche.

This photo, taken after the avalanche, shows the valley where Yungay once stood. The town has disappeared.

What happens in an avalanche?

When an avalanche happens people do not get any warning. Sometimes people report hearing a soft 'woosh' sound or a loud crack. Usually the first thing they know about it is being knocked over and carried fast down a mountainside.

'I heard a deep, muffled thunk as it fractured. Then it was like someone pulled the rug out from under me.' Bruce Tremper, dry **slab avalanche** survivor

Tumbling

Survivors of avalanches often describe being spun around so much they do not know which way is up. They say this is a bit like being in a tumble dryer full of snow and ice! The force of moving snow is so great that people cannot control the direction they are sliding. It is difficult to slow down because avalanches speed up as they move.

This snowboarder is trying to get safely out of the way of an avalanche that is moving down the slope.

Dangers

The biggest danger in an avalanche is not having enough air to breathe. When people are falling, the air is so full of snow that it is hard to breathe. If they get buried under snow, only a tiny amount of air is usually trapped with them. The danger is that it will run out before rescuers reach them.

Some people are injured when the avalanche throws chunks of ice, rocks and trees into them. Others suffer from **hypothermia** – they get so cold they become ill. Avalanches also bury buildings, cars, roads and tunnels under tonnes of snow, ice and soil.

Snowmobiles are heavy and can easily trigger slab avalanches.

What should people do in an avalanche?

These are a few things that people who get caught in an avalanche should do:

- Try to get off the moving slab of snow and ice.

- Try to grab a tree or boulder quickly before the avalanche builds up speed. This may help them to slow down their sliding.

- Keep moving, as if swimming hard, using their arms and legs. The greatest danger is to sink deeper into the snow.

- Try to clear a large space in front of their mouth before the avalanche stops. Then they will have a pocket of air to breathe.

- Before the snow settles, people should push a hand upward so that rescuers might see them. A good way of telling which way is up is to dribble some saliva (spit) – it always moves down towards the ground!

When big avalanches threaten towns amongst snowy mountains, the people who live there need to know what to do to remain safe.

Les Orres, France, 1998

On 23 January 1998, a group of students on a school trip set off for a walk on **snowshoes** in Les Orres in the French Alps. They had several guides with them and had just spent a week learning about snow sports and snow hazards. Heavy snowfall in the area meant there was risk of avalanches, but their guides still decided to go.

> *'One cannot criticize these people in such a tragic moment, but personally, I wouldn't have gone trekking today in these conditions.'* Gerard Bouchet, leader of one of the rescue teams

As the group walked up to a ridge above some woods, disaster struck. Their movements triggered a dry **slab avalanche** up to 300 metres wide, which swept the students down the slope. Rescue workers later found many of the survivors dazed and clinging to trees.

Out of the party of 42 that set out, 11 people were killed and 21 were injured in the avalanche at Les Orres. Over 150 rescue workers helped rescue survivors.

15

Who helps after an avalanche?

Avalanche victims have to be found fast because of the danger that they will run out of air. That is why trained, expert assistance is necessary in areas where avalanches are a problem.

Getting help

Rescue teams work in particular areas of the mountains. They have detailed knowledge of avalanche **terrain** – the areas where avalanches are more likely – and how to find buried victims there. They also watch for changes in the weather in mountains, and know when avalanches are more likely. When avalanches happen they organize teams of **volunteers** to help them find survivors. They work closely with emergency services such as the police.

AVALANCHE / FACTS

! Only half of all avalanche victims survive after being trapped in snow for more than 30 minutes.

Rescue teams try to get to the avalanche site quickly, often using helicopters and snowmobiles.

Finding people

Rescuers look for avalanche clues such as broken trees and mounds of snow with rubble. They also look for signs of buried people such as scattered clothing and rucksacks. Most buried people are found if rescuers can see a part of their body, such as a hand, sticking out of the snow.

Many others are found using probe lines. These are made up of rescuers spread out in a line, walking slowly and quietly forward. They gently poke long, thin poles into the snow, every 50 centimetres, to find buried people.

Transceivers

If a person who is buried in the snow is wearing a **transceiver**, he or she is more likely to receive help quickly. The transceiver sends out regular signals so that rescuers, who have receivers, can pinpoint exactly where the signals are coming from. This leads them to the avalanche victim. Many people who live and work in avalanche areas carry transceivers.

These people have formed a probe line. If one of their poles touches something, rescuers use shovels to carefully but quickly dig the victim out.

Helping dogs

Rescuers also use working dogs to find avalanche victims. Most of the dogs are German Shepherds, but some are St Bernards and labradors.

Rescue dogs are specially trained by their owners. First the dogs are trained to recognize a human's smell. Then they are trained to smell this smell through deeper and deeper snow. Most rescue dogs can find people buried up to 4 metres, but a few have found survivors under 10 metres of snow. The usual reward for these dogs is to spend some time playing with their trainer!

Sensitive noses

People always give off a faint scent because of **bacteria** growing on their skin. Dogs can smell this scent thousands of times better than people can. If someone is caught in an avalanche, their scent spreads through the snow around them. Rescue dogs search for patches of snow where the smell is strongest.

One rescue dog with its trainer can search avalanche areas about eight times faster than 20 people in probe lines.

Medical care

Once avalanche victims have been found, many need immediate first aid. Rescue teams are trained to deal with injuries such as broken limbs, cuts and knocks. They also treat **hypothermia** by gently warming the victims using special heated vests and blankets. Victims with more serious injuries are taken by helicopter to specialist hospitals where experts can treat them.

Other dangers

When avalanches hit towns or cities, large numbers of people may face other dangers. The force of an avalanche can trap people under collapsed buildings or inside cars. It can pull down **powerlines** that may **electrocute** people. Powerlines can also make sparks that start fires.

Sometimes emergency services like the police work with national forces such as the army to rescue victims. Some poorer countries have fewer rescue workers and less rescue equipment. They may ask for help from richer countries after a major avalanche disaster.

After an avalanche – or any other natural disaster – more victims will survive if emergency services can find them and help them as quickly as possible.

Anchorage, Alaska, USA, 2000

The Seward Highway is the main road connecting the cities of Anchorage and Seward in Alaska, USA. It is the route that is used for the transportation of food and other goods to people living on the Kenai peninsula. It is also one of the most avalanche-threatened roads in North America because of the high cliffs and steep slopes on either side of it.

The winter of 1999–2000 was a bad one in Alaska. Very cold weather froze the snow that had fallen. Then temperatures rose and thawed the fallen snow, making a weak layer. In January, four times the usual amount of snow fell around Anchorage. This added thousands of tonnes to the **snow cover** on top of the weak layer.

Warmer weather, high winds and rainstorms **triggered** many dry **slab avalanches**. One of these avalanches flattened buildings in the city of Cordova, causing US$2.6 million in damage. On 2 February 2000, several avalanches up to a kilometre across covered the Seward Highway, cutting off around 2000 people in Kenai. Tens of thousands of people had no electricity for a week after **powerlines** were knocked down.

The Alaskan avalanches of 1999–2000 were a major disaster affecting thousands of people.

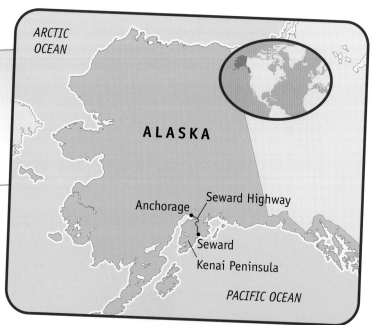

ARCTIC OCEAN

ALASKA

Anchorage

Seward Highway

Seward

Kenai Peninsula

PACIFIC OCEAN

Rescue and clear-up

National guards, police and other emergency services worked together to rescue stranded people quickly. Highway workers and **volunteers** cleared most of the Seward Highway using bulldozers and shovels.

Helicopters dropped **explosives** to clear patches of thick snow from slopes above the road. This was done to stop a big avalanche threatening the workers below. However, when three bulldozers started to clear the road of snow, strong winds above the slopes started a wind avalanche. The drivers had little warning before it hit them.

> *'I could hear the windows starting to crackle and shatter. Then one popped and so did the others.'* Larry Bushnell, bulldozer driver

Two of the bulldozer drivers were only slightly injured, but the third died. His 16-tonne machine was pushed 100 metres by the avalanche and rolled upside-down. Although they faced dangerous conditions, workers eventually managed to clear the road.

Rescue and repair workers clearing up after avalanches are often at high risk of further danger.

Can avalanches be predicted?

Many people who live in and around snowy mountains make their living from **tourism**. They provide food, hotels and lessons for winter visitors who want to ski, for example. To keep tourists safe they rely on the accurate prediction of avalanches.

Avalanche institutes

There are special avalanche **institutes** in many countries such as Japan and the USA where avalanches are a problem. Avalanche institute workers collect information about avalanche **terrain**, such as how steep mountain slopes or valleys are. They also record whether trees in woodland are close together or not. When trees are close together, they hold the fallen snow in place. When trees are far apart, avalanches can run between them. Avalanche institutes use all this information to draw avalanche hazard maps. These maps show which areas are more likely to have avalanches.

RISQUE D'AVALANCHE
PROMENADE INTERDITE

NO ENTRY
RISK OF AVALANCHE

LAWINENGEFAHR
FÜR FUSSGÄNGER VERBOTEN

STRADA VIETATA PER
RISCHIO DI VALANGA

When avalanche institutes have worked out which areas are at risk of avalanches, they can warn people about the danger.

Weather and snow cover

Avalanche institutes also collect information about the weather, and especially about snowfall. They measure how much snow falls each day, the direction the wind is blowing, and air temperature. Scientists **forecast** how the weather might change and **trigger** avalanches. They use information from photographs of clouds taken by **satellites** in space and from their knowledge of **climate**.

Scientists examine **snow cover** to see if it may avalanche. By looking at the thickness and type of snow in its layers, they can see whether it has settled tightly. Snow that has not settled tightly has air spaces in it, and sounds hollow when it is tapped.

Acid rain and avalanches

When **pollution** in the air mixes with rainwater, it makes acid rain. The acid rain then falls on trees and kills their leaves. If acid rain kills trees in avalanche areas, it means the trees cannot act like fences to stop or slow down avalanches.

Scientists look closely at snowcover in avalanche hazard areas by carefully digging holes called snow pits.

Can avalanches be prevented?

Avalanches are natural forces. People cannot stop avalanches once they are in motion, but they can prevent thick **snow cover** building up in the first place.

Looking after trees

Trees are an important way of making slopes stable. Trees are a natural barrier to avalanches and their roots also help to hold **topsoil** together. When people cut down trees for **timber** or **firewood**, the topsoil is exposed and may be washed away by rain or carried away by avalanches. Eventually this may leave a surface of bare rock. Snow cover is even less stable on bare rock.

Tree protection

Even six hundred years ago people knew that trees could stop avalanches. In forested avalanche areas of Switzerland, forest inspectors punished people for damaging trees – even for just picking their berries and cones. In the worst cases, the punishment was death.

People should only cut down a few trees from mountain slopes, so there are enough trees left to help stop avalanches.

Breaking up snow

The best way of preventing avalanches is to remove unstable snow before it becomes a hazard. Skilled people set off small, controlled avalanches. Ski **rangers** regularly visit avalanche **terrain** after heavy snowfall. They look for overhangs of snow on ridges. They test the strength of snow cover by zigzagging across slopes on skis, and jumping up and down on the snow.

Army teams use rifles and cannons to 'shoot the slopes' with **explosives**. From up to 2 kilometres away they blow up suspect snow on large slopes and overhangs. Ski rangers and mountain patrol teams sometimes use avalaunchers – special cannons powered by gas. Unlike guns they make no noise when they fire, which is better as loud noise can **trigger** an avalanche. People also use helicopters and planes to shoot the slopes in less accessible areas.

These two explosions have started a controlled avalanche on a mountain. The explosives were set off by a team travelling by helicopter.

How do people prepare for avalanches?

Not all avalanches can be prevented. This means that people who live and work in areas threatened by avalanches have to be prepared when disaster strikes.

Many villages and towns build avalanche breakers on the slopes above them. These are strong barriers that can change the direction in which an avalanche is moving. The barriers are sometimes big heaps of rock and soil. Or they may be special V-shaped concrete structures about 4 metres high and 100 metres long.

When people build their houses on a mountain, they usually give them long sloping roofs. This is because avalanches are more likely to slide over a sloping roof than knock down the house.

Some roads and railway tracks are protected from smaller avalanches by special tunnels. These are called galleries. They stop the people and vehicles inside being buried in snow and rock.

These barriers will help to trap snow that falls in winter. Then it will not slip towards the buildings further down the valley.

Personal planning

People who want to travel on snowy mountains should follow a few simple rules. They should:

- learn about the area – its weather, **snow cover**, and any dangerous areas they should avoid
- tell someone where they are going and when they will be back
- pack the right items – lots of warm clothing, a shovel, a mobile phone or a **transceiver**, and some high-energy food
- look out for areas where avalanches could happen, including open slopes and valleys, and overhanging **snowdrifts** on ridges
- look out for signs of past avalanches such as damaged trees
- travel along valley floors, through dense (crowded) trees and on slopes that are not too steep
- turn back if they see signs of unsafe snow cover.

Some people carry special airbags in their rucksacks that inflate if an avalanche hits. This helps keep the wearer near the surface of the snow – a bit like wearing a rubber ring in water.

What about avalanches in the future?

In the future, as in the past, avalanches will depend on things people have little control over, such as **snow cover** and changes in the weather. However, people can avoid being caught in avalanches by being sensible. If they follow safety rules, build in safe areas and limit the number of mountain trees they cut down, fewer people will be hurt in future.

Scientists can also help. They are developing better systems to predict avalanches. In Switzerland, electronic monitors around the country measure things like snow temperature and wind speed. They automatically send this information to a computer. This computer produces accurate avalanche **forecasts** for each part of the country. Equipment like this will mean that fewer people will be caught in avalanches in the future.

This electronic snow probe is a new tool for measuring the strength of snow layers. It is a much quicker method than digging a snow pit.

Some avalanche disasters of the past

Thousands of big avalanches happen every year. These are some of the biggest and most crushing avalanches that have happened in the past 100 years.

1910, Wellington, Washington, USA
Three trains, several carriages and a station house were pushed over the edge of a 50-metre cliff into a canyon by a spring avalanche.

1915–1918, World War I, European Alps
Avalanches claimed the lives of over 60,000 soldiers fighting in the Alps. Most avalanches happened naturally, but some may have been triggered by one side shooting into the snow-covered slopes above their enemies.

1950–51, The Winter of Terror, European Alps
Warm air from the Atlantic Ocean caused unusually high amounts of snow and rain, resulting in over 600 major avalanches. In Austria alone, thousands of acres of forest and several small villages were destroyed. One hundred people were killed.

1962, Ranrahirca, Peru
An ice avalanche near Yungay buried several villages, killing over 3000 people. (See page 10.)

1970, Val d'Isère, France
A youth hostel was destroyed by an avalanche at breakfast time. Rescuers used dinner plates to help dig out the survivors.

1999, Galteur, Austria
A 500-metre-wide avalanche hit the village of Galteur. Rescuers could not reach the village for 16 hours. They found 23 buried survivors but another 31 people who were dead.

Glossary

bacteria tiny (microscopic) living things that can cause diseases

blizzard wind-blown snowstorm

climate weather conditions that normally affect a large area over a long period of time

electrocute kill by electric shock

explosive material that blows up, suddenly releasing energy

firewood wood burnt to provide heat, often for cooking

forecast prediction

glacier huge piece of ice formed after snow falls at high altitude

hypothermia when body temperature drops so much that the person becomes ill and could die without first aid

ice avalanche avalanche caused by a large moving lump of ice

institute group or organization of people who work together to learn and teach others about something

pie chart type of graph which divides a circle into slices of different sizes to show different amounts

pollution dirt or chemicals that spoil air, land or water

powerlines main electricity cables

ranger someone who looks after a natural area, such as a forest or a national park

satellite object put into space that can send TV signals or take photographs, for example

slab avalanche avalanche caused by the break-up of heavy, solid snow cover or a slab of snow

snow cover snow that has fallen and built up on land

snowdrifts where wind has blown snow into a very big pile

snowshoes shoes like tennis racquets. They have large nets for soles, which spread the wearer's weight to stop them sinking into snow.

terrain shape of land

timber wood used for building

topsoil upper layer of soil

tourism everything to do with holidays, from the holidaymakers to the places where they stay and eat

transceiver special machine that makes a signal or message. The signal can be detected using machines called receivers.

trigger set off or start

volunteer person who offers help without being paid

wind avalanche avalanche caused by thick clouds of snow powder in the air

Find out more

Books

Nature in Action: Avalanche, Stephen Kramer (Alaska Mountain Safety Centre, 2001)

Wild Earth: Avalanche!, Lorraine Jean Hopping (Cartwheel Books/Scholastic, 2002)

Websites

www.avalanche.org/~uac/Common-questions.html – this website contains the answers to lots of common questions about avalanches.

www.pbs.org/wgbh/nova/avalanche – the website of the US TV channel PBS, which has some good avalanche information, film and pictures.

www.comdens.com/SAR – this website contains an interesting description of avalanche dog training.

www.sais.gov.uk/about_avalanches – this website contains useful information about avalanches in the UK.

Index

Titles in the *Awesome Forces of Nature* series include:

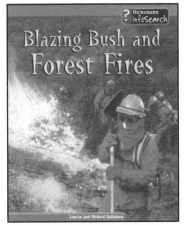

Hardback   0 431 17828 3

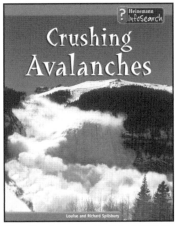

Hardback   0 431 17831 3

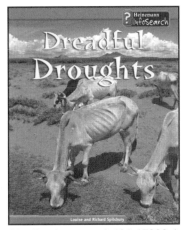

Hardback   0 431 17829 1

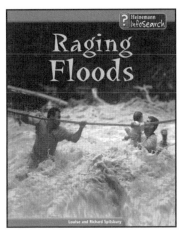

Hardback   0 431 17830 5

Hardback   0 431 17832 1

Find out about the other titles in this series on our website www.heinemann.co.uk/library